MY DEEPEST HEART'S DEVOTIONS 6

AN AFRICAN WOMAN'S DIARY - BOOK 6

GERTRUDE KABATALEMWA

Edited by NONA BABICH AND TERESA SKINNER
Photography by ALISA ALBERS
Photography by TERESA SKINNER

ISBN: 978-1-950123-27-8

Copyright © 2019 by Teresa Skinner

Unless otherwise indicated, all Scripture quotations are taken from the Holy Bible, King James Version - Public Domain Scripture quotations marked (ESV) ® Bible (The Holy Bible, English Standard Version®), copyright © 2001 by Crossway, a publishing ministry of Good News Publishers. Used by permission. All rights reserved."

Scripture quotations marked (NIV) are taken from the Holy Bible, New International Version®, NIV®. Copyright © 1973, 1978, 1984, 2011 by Biblica, Inc.™ Used by permission of Zondervan. All rights reserved worldwide. www.zondervan.com The "NIV" and "New International Version" are trademarks registered in the United States Patent and Trademark Office by Biblica, Inc.™

All rights reserved.

No part of this book may be reproduced in any form or by any electronic or mechanical means, including information storage and retrieval systems, without written permission from the publisher, except for the use of brief quotations in a book review.

*Gone so soon,
with all the dedicated work she had done...
we will continue with the work she has left behind.
showing people "God's Love and Care"
Emmanuel Mwesigye*

CONTENTS

Foreword   xi

1. Aidah's Testimony   1
2. "Guess Who?"   5
3. Who is He?   9
4. The Lord Asked Me My Priorities   13
5. What Do Unbelievers of the World "See"   17
6. He is Our Joy and Our Peace   23
7. Why Such a Large Sand Area?   27
8. Mark People You Call Your Friends   29
9. Can We Build Three Huts?   35
10. I Am Asking, "Lord, Be My Friend?"   39
11. What is a Plate?   45
12. No Compromise   49
13. Give Time to Daily Prayer   53
14. He Will Have People Who Will Praise, Pray and Worship   59
15. A Spiritual Measuring Line   63
16. Lord Clothe Me with a Robe of Prayer   67
17. Thoughts   71
18. Influence   75
19. We Have the Opportunity to Become Radiant Christians   79

Acknowledgments   85
About the Author   87

WORD OF THE LORD FOR GERTRUDE KABATALEMWA

I believe I heard the Lord say
You are a General - in His army
You are a woman of valor
You are a woman of great faith
Those who have preceded you and those that will follow

There is not one with a greater faith as you
You are an Apostle - there will be more churches established
Training up those in your care now to begin other church groups
As His message of salvation and love continues to be spread
throughout the nation

I believe I heard the Lord say
Your job is not done
You have accomplished much but
There is much more to be accomplished
He has given you a great vision
And those to stand with you in bringing forth this vision
You cannot do this alone

I believe I heard Him say
Begin to seek Him
There are those who are now working in various projects
But He will begin to show you - one by one-
Those whom He will raise up to walk beside you
To further along and to fulfill the vision
Walking with you in unity, harmony and one accord
To accomplish the same vision He has given you
You to delegate responsibility for various projects to those He shows you
So that you can be freed up to begin new endeavors
And to further along others

Multiplication - multiplication of help - more people to be set in place to help you
To take on more of the work that needs to be done
Delegation - your delegating more work to others to free up yourself

He will continue to provide for you
Finances help in all you need
The vision is expanding
More will be started
More will be accomplished

And I believe I hear the Lord say
The angels of the Lord encamp around you
And continue to be at your side
To protect you and provide for the needs
Rest in peace knowing that even greater things are in store
Greater things will be accomplished

And I believe I hear the Lord say

You have been found faithful
He loves you very much

And the Lord says to you
"Well done My good and faithful servant!"

Sunday Mar 28, 2010 Approximately 5:20 PM

FOREWORD

We may not agree with what Ms. Gertrude Kabatalemwa has written. It may not be politically correct for our generation. But, let us get passed our judgements, and hear the heart of this African woman.

If so, we will find ourselves understanding a depth of spirituality that will most likely be lost to the next generations.

AFRICA HAS SOMETHING TO SAY TO US.

May we listen intently with raw ears to hear a direction that could keep our future from becoming sterile.

Teresa Skinner
All Nations International

CHAPTER 1

AIDAH'S TESTIMONY

AIDAH'S TESTIMONY, the angels replied, "There are seven things one must do to build up their materials to build their home.

The first is their accumulation of worship and praise to God. The second is their time spent reading the Bible. The third is their time spent praying. The fourth is their time spent evangelizing people. The fifth is giving one's offering to the Lord. The sixth is their obedient tithing to God. And seventh, lastly, their time spent serving the church. These are the deeds or works of obedience in which one accumulates materials for their Heavenly home. If one is lacking in these areas, they will have no materials to build their home.

Testimony of Heaven by Margaret O. Amure. She saw many pastors' mansions in heaven that were not even finished yet, although they had been in ministry for many years. She said their homes were barely started; some only had a foundation or not much more than a first floor. She asked, and was told it is because they did not send up building materials. When you build a foundation on earth through your good works, you send up materials for your mansion's foundation in heaven. If there are no materials being sent up, then they cannot build your mansion and the work stops. You determine while you are on earth what materials they will use to build your mansion in heaven. *4th August 2013*

AIDAH'S TESTIMONY, HERE ON EARTH EVERYONE HAS HIS 'tube' or something like a 'pipe.' It is not only believers who have it but it is the same for every one whether saved or not. Every person has his own 'tube' which goes up to heaven; and note that what I am saying here is what the Lord sent me to say, and it applies to every human being. God is the one who created every one whether you believe in Him or not. You will be responsible to God and you will answer on that day whether you take these things seriously or not. Whether you have decided to practice witchcraft or not, you will meet God and will have to answer. That is why the Word of God says that blessed are those who die in Jesus Christ. All our deeds follow us. For some people their deeds go shouting following them as they leave earth after death.

Everyone has tube which connects to heaven. It is like the example of the mouth; each one has his own mouth. But just as some people do not use their mouths, in the same way some people do not use their 'tubes.' It is the devil who makes things to be misused or unused. Everyone who is a human being has 'tube' or 'pipe.' Every word or thought goes through your personal pipe and it connects in heaven to your personal phone. This pipe is connected by a system and they connect you to your personal phone. Everything that goes through these pipes and phones goes to the concerned department in heaven. Every individual on earth has their phone in heaven.

These 'tubes' resemble the medium plastic pipes which are used here on earth in houses or in making toilets to carry water.

The phones are on a pole in heaven; this pole is like the poles that people make here on earth when constructing storied buildings. There is a huge pole in heaven on which the phones of every one on earth are found. The pole has four sides and it is sparkling white. Every individual on earth has phone on that pole. Each individual's phone place also has your number; it has the day that you were placed in your mother's womb; it has your birth date. It also has your history and lineage from your ancestors up to you.

Now imagine that you are here in the studio and you think like this, "I am busy now but after, I will go home at 11.00pm and at 11.25pm I will pray." As you think that thought in your heart here on earth, in heaven they hear every bit of it loudly the way you would hear loud sound from very big speakers here on earth. In heaven there is no difference between words, thoughts, secrets, etc. They are heard as loudly as a loud speaker announced them all over heaven. Immediately the angels that are concerned start getting ready to receive your prayer. They get ready and wait for your prayer at that exact time. I saw that because of these angels are made to move up and down a lot to go by human beings. This is because people think a lot and they speak or talk a lot but they rarely put those thoughts or words into actions. If you thought of praying at a given time and in a given place, the angels will get ready and wait there for you. The angels do not miss the time; they do not add or subtract on the time you decided or thought about in your heart.

Angels are made to move up and down a lot because people think and talk a lot but they act very rarely; they do very little. Very thought or word is an order to the angels in heaven. The moment you think of it, they get ready to receive the prayer, i.e. someone tells you that there is a pastor that prays on radio at such a time.

If you decide in your heart that you will pray with that pastor at that time on the radio; let's say at 11.40 o'clock, the moment you think that in your heart, angels get to work on that issue; immediately a file is opened on the issue. If on that day angels come and find you not where you at decided to pray at home, they will wait there and it will be charged against you. In case you have been diverted by an emergency, it is still expected of you to carry out what you had decided in your thoughts at the exact time you set in your heart. If you fail it is charged against you. So, if you do not mean to carry out something, do not think about doing it nor talk about or say it out.

"To understand the present and anticipate the future, one must know the past, enough to have a sense of the history of a people."

FORMER SINGAPORE PREMIER, LEE KWAN YEW

His analysis must be taken seriously. *25th August 2013*

CHAPTER 2

"GUESS WHO?"

JESUS SEEING their faith said to the paralytic "Son, your sins are forgiven," Mark 2:5. The scribes were reasoning in their hearts, but Jesus could see in the hearts of men. He answered them accordingly. The Pharisees were criticizing the Lords disciples for picking the grain and rubbing it in their hands on a Sabbath. Jesus said to them the Sabbath was made for man, not man for the Sabbath, Mark 2:27. *1st September 2013*

THE LORD GOD COMMANDED THE HIGH PRIESTS NOT TO DO these rituals because we are the Priesthood and a chosen nation; defilement by touching, viewing dead bodies, not cutting our bodies (tattooing), not to shave off all our hair (shawulin), Leviticus 21, 22. *2nd September 2013*

OUR LORD DID THE FOLLOWING: THE DEMONS IN THE MAD man recognized the Lord but people could not recognize Him at all, He healed the mad man of Gadara, Mark 5:1-17.

He healed the woman with an issue of blood; our Lord recognized the power went out of Him, even though His disciples tried to draw His attention away, Mark 5:24-34. This is how the world tries to reason what God is doing.

He healed the daughter of Jairus did not give up even though when they told him his daughter Had died and shouldn't disturb the Lord, but he trusted the Lord and hanged on His Word "Do not be afraid only believe," He told Jairus, when he went to the house of Jairus He did not allow the crowd to go with Him. He went with the few who had faith in Him. Times when people do not have any positive attitude towards situations and what you are doing do not help but they come as spectators, Mark 5:21-43.

6th September 2013

MY EXPERIENCES:

In the 1980s He carried me and we went and sat on an Island. He snapped His finger and I saw a star running as it ran it brought part of Italy's sea shore close to us and He told me how dangerous that place was. When I asked Him that I had never seen how He smiled and I was wondering that when He was on the earth I never saw Him laughing in all the paintings man drew. This time He took me to heaven and I saw all the saints in heaven as they were walking behind the big glass door and passing by some recognized me. Then our Lord came also behind that glass and He smiled at me and I was so excited to see Him smile.

When I was living at Prince Charles Drive in Kololo I was really going through big trials. The Lord came in the Morning when we were in the woods. He sat on the big log and started humming a song for me, one I had never heard before. "It is So Sweet to Trust in Jesus" when I came out of that vision, I kept humming it too. But later it disappeared and I cried Lord it has disappeared and I was disappointed. He said do not worry when it's the right time it will return. After a few months I was invited to All Saints Church for Fellowship, and that song was sung and the Lord reminded me that that was the song He Hummed for me.

I had a dream, our Lord was walking with me and we were conversing, but Mr Nkurukenzire came towards us when I turn to look at our Lord to see if Nkurukenzire had seen Him, instead there was a boy sucking his thumb. I asked the Lord why He did that. He said that how some people they see Him, like a little boy.

In March 2010, we went to visit Bro Thad with Sis Judi Zak. Early in the Morning the Lord came, when I saw Him and recognized Him, He winked at me to say, do not say. He went around and blind folded Thad with His hands to ask him "Guess Who?" He was looking at me to say do not tell Him Who I am; and He told me "I love Thad very much."

> *Memory, on 29th April 2012 I had a vision that our Lord was showing His wounded hands to people around me, one by one, when He reached me He passed me by and I asked Him why He did not show me.*

> *He said; for you have already seen them.* 7th September 2013

CHAPTER 3

WHO IS HE?

AFTER THE PHARISEES and scribes coming from Jerusalem thought that they were so holy, they went on to despise the disciples of our Lord gossiping that the disciples were eating with Impure hands that is without washing their hands.

Yes, many times people think they have been somewhere, e.g. in the church on a mountain praying, fasting, and giving to the poor, etc. they think that they are holier than those who went nowhere. In actual fact some people who go nowhere you find they are the ones walking with the Lord. When you judge and despise people the Lord asks rightly did Isaiah prophesy of you hypocrites? People honor me with their lips, but their hearts are far away from me.

After hearing Him the Syrophoenician woman kept asking Him to cast the demons out of her daughter, but our Lord was saying to her: let the children be satisfied first, when the woman said even dogs sit under the table and eat the children's crumbs. Because of this answer our Lord said to her, "Go, the demons have left your daughter." This reminds me of the Word that "He sends His Word and it heals them," Matthew 8:5-13.

So shall my word be that goeth forth out of my mouth: it shall not return unto me void, but it shall accomplish that which I please, and it shall. Isaiah 55:11

Because of incredible miracles the disciple's hearts were hardened! Not softened?

On that day, when evening had come, he said to them, "Let us go across to the other side." And leaving the crowd, they took him. Mark 4:35-41 (ESV).

He said: come out of the man you unclean spirit, the madman of Gadara, Mark 5:8.

He said Daughter your faith has made you well, and blood issue woman, Mark 5:34.

He said "Talitha Koum" means "Little girl I say to you get up," Mark 5:41.

He said you give them something to eat, all they could find was 5 bread and 2 fish yet 5,000 people ate and 12 baskets were left over, Mark 6:37-44.

He said "it is I, do not be afraid" as He walked on water, Mark 6:50.

He said "Ephphatha!" this means "Be opened!" to a deaf and dumb boy who was brought to him, Mark 7:34-36.

He said "I feel compassion," with 7 bread loaves and a few fish 4,000 people ate, Mark 8. *8th September 2013*

HE BEGAN TO TEACH AND SAID TO THEM: IS IT NOT WRITTEN that my house shall be called house of prayer for all nations? But you have made it a robber's den? The Chief Priests and the scribes, heard this and began seeking how to destroy Him, for they were afraid of Him, Mark 11:17-18.

It is of today the Churches have been turned into stock markets, flea markets, and show halls where women go to show fashions. They are entertainment halls with music men and women in Mass Choirs who have to go for makeup early before the service and they dress in worldly fashions. Women come to church dressed indecently competing with each other. Young women and men come not to seek God but to seek partners. The church is no longer respected because that is where the High Priests and Scribes make deals and appointments saying "come and we will meet at the church after church service we will meet."

So the High Priests and scribes were seeking how to destroy Him because He was saying the truth. Even now if you speak the truth in the church and point out the errors of the Pastors then you will be excommunicated. *11th September 2013*

CHAPTER 4

THE LORD ASKED ME MY PRIORITIES

I WOKE up to pray before leaving for the village. As I was Walking and Counting the years where the Lord has passed me through with my two boys Peter and Robert. Peter, it was 1979-2001 disappeared and returned of Peter and 2001 - 2013 He has had no job and he is not living as he should live. So, 22+12 = 34 years. Robert, it was 2003-2013 when he disappeared and returned in 11 years. Totals = 45 years of trials. From October 2nd-16th November I was led to fast on 2 cups of Water and Honey, and I completed this fast for 45 days. Lord, does it **have a the signif**icance of these 45 years?

This morning I left for the village with Emma, Peter and Stephanie.

16th September 2013

I am a missionary on a mission; I will not leave

> ***until the mission is*** *accomplished and I am not a missionary on a mission that can retire before the mission is finished!* 18th September 2013

KATOORA EHA!!! NYOWE NKATOORA ENTE!

This came when I was praying for Uganda and our leaders. I remembered a Libyan president who had cloned himself with so many others, his people did not know who exactly who was with them, the real president or a cloned one. When the time of war came and he had to die the Lord knew exactly who was the real one. I liked it because it was like when we were young and played the game of "Guess Where Is The Cow?"

(Katoora Eha, Nyowe nk**atora e**nte). So, the real Gaddafi was picked and killed. The Lord picked the fist with the cow. Our Leaders forget so quickly!

Prayer, Lord, help our Nation with the foolishness of our lead**ers who are like ost**rich as they bury their heads in the sand and think that the people are not seeing what they are doing. Amen. *21st September 2013*

THE LORD ASKED ME MY PRIORITIES. I ASKED TO WALK IN His presence daily until He returns or calls me home, I asked for great wisdom to counsel kings and rulers and His people, and I asked to know His Word. Knowing God intimately is all in all, because you are in His presence all the time, and when you are in His Presence whatever you desire, need and want are there. God is not like a man because He sees even your thoughts and gives

You your heart's desires. When Solomon asked for wisdom God gave him that also He had given him even what he did not ask for. God knows how my heart aches for my son Robert because He has promised to return him several times. He knows Peter does not have a job and why he has kept him on the broad. He knows why I need the school buildings and other facilities at Nyamabuga and Amber House. He knows I am not asking for a mansion for myself, **it is for His se**rvice and these are not asked in innuendo or with a motive behind them which would exalt myself. Thank you, Lord. 25th September 2013

I RETURNED FROM THE VILLAGE ON 27TH AND DECIDED TO rest at home. Once again, the Lord spoke of what He told me earlier about moving, I have completely forgotten about this since He was talking of it in 2010 while I was still at Annet's house. I was rolling the house rugs when He said to keep them rolled until we shift and is said I still have most of the things packed. He said most will go to the village.

He said I have been asking about the 45 days fast. Will they still have their full impact? Why were they appointed?

I have been asking about the great heaven visitation of Ann Rountree. Now I know that each child of God has a special place in God's heart. She was called to accomplish that task, where she also can stand in awe but not accomplish, and we also have ours, He talked about not Uganda, not East Africa, but the continent of Africa referring to a message He gave me about that account in 2011.

How can a helicopter be promised without a task? To save distance and time and in order to meet deadlines is task.

I have prepared you for the end-time duty you are play,

because it's you to play it for me for I have ordained you for it. I know it's you who can play that role for me.

He called a name "Burungi-buliza." 28th September 2013

School and evangelism van

CHAPTER 5

WHAT DO UNBELIEVERS OF THE WORLD "SEE"

AT 11.00 PM IN Pastor Sserwadda's sermon about how he left a rented house.

INSIDE ME I said "SSERWADDA IS SSERWADDA, I AM Kabatalemwa. Kabatalemwa cannot be Sserwadda and Sserwadda cannot be Kabatalemwa. What I have gone through Sserwadda cannot go through them, and what Sserwadda has gone through I cannot go through them.

Heaven speaks, When Jesus said that He was in the Father, and you, meaning the apostles, were in Him. The apostles had been with Jesus, and had advanced to this point, where Jesus could say this. At that day ye shall know that I am in my Father, and ye in me, and I in you, John 14:20. They had operated under the power of God, ministering miracles, through the authority of Jesus, and were ready to lay down their lives for Him.

However, could Jesus say the same thing about us today? The secret was that they had become "in" Jesus; i.e. toys that are "in" each other, I have a wooden Russian toy that has 6 parts. Each part is a smaller one than the next size up that it fits inside of and this fitting inside continues until all smaller ones are hidden inside of the biggest one. Once assembled all you can see is the biggest one. The smaller ones are "in" the biggest one, and the tiniest one is the most hidden. They are all hidden and invisible to the eye. They have become "one" toy. I wonder if this could represent "oneness" that many people debate over, with regard to God? This is just my theory, and something to think about.

What do unbelievers of the world or other believers "see" when they look at us?

When others look at us, who should be true believers, all they should see is God. True believers are completely covered by the glory of Jesus, who is completely covered by the glory of the Father God. We should be the center, most hidden piece, like the tiniest piece in the Russian toy. Being under God's covering does not make us God. It just means we are "in" Him and receive His protection and spirit, and are totally in line with His perfect will.

If all people really "see" is us then we are drawing attention to ourselves instead of to God. We are exposed and spiritually naked without the covering of Jesus which is required to obtain the covering of our Father God. This also means that it is easier for the devil to attack us, since we are not covered.

We should be the most "hidden" piece. It is like we do not exist to the world. Our "self" has died and all that is left is Jesus who also has died, so that all look like the Father. The plan is to glorify God, not ourselves. This is our greatest freedom, when we have gotten to this level, even though we have to "die to self" to get there. We have to die to ourselves, therefore, in that we will be in Jesus and Jesus will be in the Father, so when the enemy tries to see us, he will see our Father

How to die to self? The price is very high. You will feel much sorrow and abandonment during this process. You will be lonely, despised, disgraced, misunderstood, falsely accused, rejected, and criticized. You will be back stabbed. You will wish at times that you had never been born. You will feel like God abandoned you, as you watch others being blessed. Your own family may ignore and reject you, and mistreat you. You may not have a friend in the world. The price may be your honor, acceptance, public standing, personal value in the eyes of the world, and possibly the church.

You will lose any level of wealth you have, and success in life may never come. All your good works may be called evil. You will give, and give, and give to others and do many good works. And No One will care about you. You will be constantly overlooked, and more carnal, less qualified, people will be chosen in your place. People will push you aside as if you are nothing, and run to others instead. If you need help, no one will help you, or care if you die. Why do people ignore you? Because you are fading away, and not demanding attention. They cannot "see" you anymore. Many times, you will feel ashamed and a failure. There will be many things you will not be able to have. Once you are detached from the painful emotions that you will experience all you can feel is the love of God for those who hate you sharing God's pain, and yours is the constant need to be alone with God, and no one else, you are dead. You no longer care about worldly things. Sometimes you forget yourself that you even exist. Yes.

Are you ready for this? Submit to God - totally. What you want is nothing. He **will provide if you** submit. He already knows what you need. If you are totally submitted, what you need will be provided, even without having to ask, although asking is ok. *29th September 2013*

HE ASKED "WHAT ARE YOUR PRIORITIES?" I SAID I WANT TO

resist the devil and his temptations, especially to pride, worldly things, and carnal things. Yes, this is hard. May I turn my back on my sins and not keep repeating them. Yes. I do not even desire material things, except for necessities. May I be nonmaterialistic in your thinking and behavior. When I want to know what is necessary may I just look at what Jesus had and did not have. I know He said "He was poor that we may be rich." For ye know the grace of our Lord Jesus Christ, that, though he was rich, yet for your sakes he became poor, that ye through his poverty might be rich, 2 Corinthians 8:9. Let me have them, but I may not regard them more important, may not be consumed by them. Many people are in need, when I have them, I will rescue many out of situations. May I give to the poor and needy as much as possible. Give me the grace Lord to identify the poor and the needy whom I am to bless. I want to put others first. I am not the center of the universe. May I continue to help to bring salvation people of, all colors, languages and nations. I do not demand, or crave, attention or "credit" for what you do God. The world is His stage, not mine.

Help me Lord to keep under your wings, Psalm 91.

I want to be a hidden vessel. Let my good works be a secret as much as possible. As long as You are "increased" in honor Jesus and I am "decreased." I must allow myself to decrease so that Jesus is increased. This is what John the Baptist and the apostles did. I should follow their example. I agree to these desires here, that the Lord may grant me these attributes. This may really hurt, but do not protest when others ignore you or slight you. Not just the world, but other believers may do this, if they are in the flesh. This is God working in your life, to humble you. I have gone through this for such a long time. May the Lord help me to keep me from protesting. I want to read the Word of God every day. I cannot live spiritually without being nourished with the Word, if I avoid this, I lose my inner peace, and become a "dry bone." True the Word enriches me. May I spend more and more time with God each day, until I get to the point that it is anguish to be away from Him. I am working on being in His presence daily.

Allow me to avoid trouble if at all possible, but accept persecution for my faith or good works. I am going deeper in God. I do that most of the time. May I spend time in personal praise and worship. Trying that with the Inner Man with time I will be there

Let me evaluate carefully every word preacher say. There are many good ones out there, and then there are some real fakes. May I be sure their words lines up with the word of God. I do not want to just accept what they read to me. I will read the passage in context to be sure they are giving me the proper interpretation. Yes I will do and go back and read for myself. I want to feel the being "in Christ" before the world. I want that very much. If the world likes you and does not bother you, you are not dead yet. You are "one" with the world. You are not invisible due to a lack of covering. If you are "in Jesus," it will be like you do not exist, even to yourself, and all anyone see is God. Since people of the world "hate" Jesus, and also His Father God, they will persecute what they see, because they hate the Jesus, your covering is that what they see.

True, this I have seen many times. Since Jesus was "in the Father," when Jesus was here, in front the disbelieving leadership all they could see was His Father God because Jesus was also dead to self. Since they secretly did not know or adore God as they should have, all they could see was someone they did not believe in, who was God Himself. Yes, they hated Jesus so much. That is why Jesus said, "when you see me, you will see the Father." He was not saying He was the Father. He was saying His Father covered Him, and he was not the one to be seen. This is also why Jesus said He who hates me hates my Father as well, John 15:23.

All they could see was His Father, when they looked at Him, so they hated Him. They were possessed by the enemy who hates God because He chased enemies from heaven, i.e. if we are yellow, Jesus is green, Father is red. If we are genuinely "in Jesus," then when someone looks at us all they will see is red. They will not see yellow or green. All you see is who is on the outside because the others are "inside." This is "Oneness." The Oneness glorifies the Father God who is the source of all power, authority, love, and glory. Yes, give it to me Lord.

Women and spiritual coverings, It is biblical for godly husbands to be an earthly covering for their wives, as they are "in Christ," who is their covering. This demonstrates the "Oneness" that is in heaven. For single women, they have only a covering that should be Jesus. They **do not need to look** to any man, or a church, for a covering. I might be able to write more about the oneness concept in a separate post. I do not want this one to get too long. Excellent. *25th September 2013*

CHAPTER 6

HE IS OUR JOY AND OUR PEACE

AS WE WERE APPROACHING HOME a prayer came to me. Lord, the enemy is causing your people to hate themselves, frustrating them until when they start asking themselves:

Why am I living? He steals their joy, their peace, and they hate even what they are doing because they see others are progressing in all what they are doing, but for them they are going nowhere.

The Word came to me that we are living for and with the king. Who lives close or near an earthly king or president and is not excited? Every day brings excitement. For us also, as long as we live with the King of kings there is excitement, joy and peace beyond human understanding because He is our Joy and our Peace, he gives us Hope every new day. I started singing as I entered the house.

30th September 2013

I WENT TO SLEEP LAST NIGHT BUT WAS IN SUCH A MESS. THE

enemy attacked me before I got to sleep, then I sought the Lord with inner intercession and He rescued me. I fought within Holy Spirit to spirit battling with scriptures, claiming every centimeter of my body and dedicating it to the Lord. The Lord heard my pleas and He came and intercepted the evil one. We need to be prepared all the time, armed with the word of God to live in His presence.

I woke up very early by 5:30am and was meditating. Children of God can kill themselves by ignorance or disobedience. When they reach heaven the Lord will ask them "Why are you here, it was not yet your time? Because of ignorance or disobedience they have cut their days short." What a loss! You may not go to hell but you would have missed something great, the accomplishment of the task the Lord created you complete on the earth. Lord let me be all the time in your presence. *1st October 2013*

I STAYED AT HOME FEELING DIZZY AND WEAK IN THE BODY.

340,000 Fighting men defected to David's Camp, this touched me;

David went out to meet them and said to them, "If you have come to me in friendship to help me, my heart will be joined to you; but if to betray me to my adversaries, although there is no wrong in my hands, then may the God of our fathers see and rebuke you... For from day to day men came to David to help him, until there was a great army, like an army of God. 1 Chronicles 12:17, 22 (ESV).*2nd October 2013*

GOD HAD BLESSED SOLOMON THUS:

¹¹ When your days are fulfilled to walk with your fathers, I will raise up your offspring after you, one of your own sons, and I will establish his kingdom. ¹² He shall build a house for me, and I will establish his throne forever. ¹³ I will be to him a father, and he shall be to me a son. I will not take my steadfast love from him, as I took it from him who was before you, ¹⁴ but I will confirm him in my house and in my kingdom forever, and his throne shall be established forever.' 1 Chronicles 17:11-14 (ESV).

3rd October 2013

CHAPTER 7

WHY SUCH A LARGE SAND AREA?

WHEN I WAS WORKING on beadwork, I conceived the idea of opening a beadwork shop with all the pieces I have ever made and will teach girls to make each design. Great Idea!!!

"I suppose so," I said quietly. I did not want to admit it, but she was right. I had wanted a home and financial security and to accomplish something for God, of course, but I had tunnel vision for the life on earth. I had Christianized the gospel of the world and bought into my own packaging. It was a bitter thing to hear that the focus of my life had been fleshly and worthless to God, and that I had not gotten away with it. "Do you want to play?" she continued cheerily. I felt a little sick. I thought I would change the subject.

Why such a large sand area?" I asked. "Many want

to build on sand, so we let them. It gets it out of their systems, you know. Maybe if you build on the sand right now, you would feel you've done that." "It seems a silly thing to do," I said stonily. "Well, yes, it does. However, building on the earth is really the same: silly toys that are long forgotten here, toys that do not even gather dust in the attic but disintegrate and are totally forgotten here, a waste of God's precious time," she said much too breezily.

HEAVEN AWAITS THE BRIDE: A
BREATHTAKING GLIMPSE OF ETERNITY
- ANNA ROUNTREE

4TH OCTOBER 2013

CHAPTER 8

MARK PEOPLE YOU CALL YOUR FRIENDS

WISDOM SPOKE to me at 7.00am.

EIGHT TO SEVEN DAYS JOURNEY WITH FOOD. WHEN DOES IT start? It has already started. 2 Chronicles 16:7-9 *5th October 2013*

JEHOSHAPHAT WAS A GOOD MAN WHO FEARED GOD, HE WAS the son of Asa, Asa was son of Ahijah, Ahijah wasson of Reheboam, Reheboam was son of Solomon, Solomon was son of David.

So Ahab was the king of Israel which was torn off from Judah because Solomon disobeyed God and married foreign women who led him away from God and he started to worship idols of other nations. Ahab was such a mess, he married Jezebel the wicked woman who killed Naboth because of his vine yard and God was so annoyed. She worshiped Baal. Ahab had more 400 prophets who were false prophets and already prophet Elijah had killed 450 when they failed to call fire to burn their sacrifices.

So the king of Israel brought together the prophets—four hundred men—and asked them, "Shall we go to war against Ramoth Gilead, or shall I not?"

"Go up, for God will give it into the hand of the king." [6] But Jehoshaphat said, "Is there not here another prophet of the Lord of whom we may inquire?" [7] And the king of Israel said to Jehoshaphat, "There is yet one man by whom we may inquire of the Lord, Micaiah the son of Imlah; but I hate him, for he never prophesies good concerning me, but always evil." And Jehoshaphat said, "Let not the king say so." [8] Then the king of Israel summoned an officer and said, "Bring quickly Micaiah the son of Imlah." 2 Chronicles 18:5-8 (ESV).

In the whole of Israel only Micaiah was a true prophet of God. He prophesied the truth and indeed Ahab was killed in that battle.

So the king of Israel brought together the prophets—four hundred men—and asked them, "Shall we go to war against Ramoth Gilead, or shall I not?"

"Go," they answered, "for God will give it into the king's hand."

The messenger who had gone to summon Micaiah said to him, "Look, the other prophets without exception are predicting success for the king. Let your word agree with theirs, and speak favorably."

But Micaiah said, "Then the king of Israel gathered the prophets together, four hundred men, and said to them, "Shall we go to battle against Ramoth-gilead, or shall I refrain?" And they said, "Go up, for God will give it into the hand of the king." 2 Chronicles 18:5, 12-13 (ESV).

"And when he had come to the king, the king said to him, "Micaiah, shall we go to Ramoth-gilead to battle, or shall I refrain?" And he answered, "Go up and triumph; they will be given into your hand." ¹⁵ But the king said to him, "How many times shall I make you swear that you speak to me nothing but the truth in the name of the Lord?" ¹⁶ And he said, "I saw all Israel scattered on the mountains, as sheep that have no shepherd. And the Lord said, 'These have no master; let each return to his home in peace.'" 2 Chronicles 18:14-16 (ESV).

Ahab wanted Micaiah to lie him in the name of the Lord as his false prophets, but instead he told him the truth. And the Lord said, One suggested this, and another that, the Lord had determined Ahab to die.

¹⁹ And the Lord said, 'Who will entice Ahab the king of Israel, that he may go up and fall at Ramoth-gilead?' And one said one thing, and another said another. ²⁰ Then a spirit came forward and stood before the Lord, saying, 'I will entice him.' And the Lord said to him, 'By what means?' ²¹ And he said, 'I will go out, and will be a lying spirit in the mouth of all his prophets.' And he said, 'You are to entice him, and you shall succeed; go out and do so.' 2 Chronicles 18:19-21 (ESV).

The deceiving spirit could enter the false prophets to make Ahab believe their lies cause the door was open in him to believe lies, not the truth, that's is why he could not listen to Micaiah. Then Zedekiah son of Kenaanah went up and slapped Micaiah in the face. "Which way did the spirit from the Lord go when he went from me to speak to you?" he asked. Micaiah replied, "You will find out on the day you go to hide in an inner room," 2 Chronicles 18:5, 23-24 (NIV).

Zedekiah a false prophet did not know how the Spirit of the Lord operates he thought is like a human being to be in one place at a time yet God's Spirit is everywhere and can operate on everyone at the same time. Micaiah assured him that he will hide in an inner room, spoken word was sent to heaven by Micaiah. "This is what the king says: Put this fellow in prison and give him nothing but bread and water until I return safely." Micaiah declared, "If you ever return safely, the Lord has not spoken through me." Then he added, "Mark my words, all you people!" 2 Chronicles 18:26-27 (NIV).

Ahab sent Micaiah to the city mayor and his son to put him in prison. Micaiah was still sticking on the word of God that "Mark my words, all you people if he goes ... "

"I will enter the battle in disguise, but you wear your royal robes." So, the king of Israel disguised himself and went into battle. Now the king of Aram had ordered his chariot commanders, "Do not Fight with anyone, small or great, except the king of Israel," 2 Chronicles 18:29-30 (NIV).

Mark people you call your friends. The devil wanted Jehoshaphat to be killed using Ahab his "so called" friend who advised him to dress as the king, whereas the king himself got disguised. Could Jehoshaphat see that? Now the king of Aram had ordered his chariot commanders, "Do not Fight with anyone, small or great, except the king of Israel." When the chariot commanders saw Jehoshaphat, they thought, "This is the king of Israel." So, they turned to attack him, but Jehoshaphat cried out, and the Lord helped him. God drew them away from him, for when the chariot commanders saw that he was not the king of Israel, they stopped pursuing him, 2 Chronicles 18:29-32 (NIV).

Because of the uprightness of Jehoshaphat the Lord helped him, and drew the chariot commanders and saw that he was not the king of Israel, so they were drawn away from him, and stopped pursuing him. Never ever trust even your closest friend, they can betray you, e.g. Ronnie & Cyrus, and Daisy.

By sunset Ahab was a dead man as Micaiah had prophesied. The Word of God can never go out of His mouth and come back void. Jehu the seer, the son of Hanani, went out to meet him and said to the king, "Should you help the wicked and love those who hate the Lord? Because of this, the wrath of the Lord is on you," 2

Chronicles 19:2 (NIV). The Lord was not happy with Jehoshaphat at all. *6th October 2013*

Craft Show in the US with Gertrude Kabatalemwa

Students dancing for visitors

Playing drums at school event

CHAPTER 9

CAN WE BUILD THREE HUTS?

MYLES MONROE TEACHING from the time of Moses to the time of John the Baptist the law was breached meaning Jesus Christ had to Come and be with us. All the books from Genesis to Malachi are of talking about the coming of Jesus Christ, but from Matthew to Revelations books are talking of Jesus. Jesus' transfiguration was Jesus' transaction. Jesus appeared with Moses and Elijah. Moses representing the Law, and Elijah the Prophesy, so the law and prophesy were closed and all ended in Jesus Christ.

PETER ASKED: CAN WE BUILD THREE HUTS FOR MOSES, Elijah and You, so that we can stay here? Myles said that's how people are building on dead people's doctrines. Jesus walked His Individual walk. Jesus did not put on their high priestly attire, He knew the devil had power over them, He did not belong to their synagogues, He was not a Sadducee, a pharisee nor a scribe. He knew the devil had infiltrated them and they were weak. He wore

His own attire, had His own teaching from heaven. Because He was an individual and did not join them, they hated Him.

Even you, if you have your own way of seeking the Lord, you keep to yourself on the word, you talk of righteousness, heaven, your dress code is different, you do not join their groups. They will try to find out where you belong. If they do not find any they will hate you.

I read the scandal of a pastor and his wife. Their church's siphoned money from the people to boost the wife's business. The wife sang in night clubs and was in sex and murder movies and while they were promoting Christianity into the secular world they lived in fashion, stylish and cool terms. They preached that God is a God of plenty and of no short change.

These are typical in the materialistic churches in the world today. Jesus says "Get out of them." *6th October 2013*

SAMUEL AND SUSANNA WESLEY HAD 19 CHILDREN IN THEIR lifetime. 11 of which died in their infancy. Samuel was an Anglican Pastor in the small town of Epworth. One night an angry church member set fire to the parsonage. Fortunately, the Wesley's were awakened by the blaze and were able to rush their children out of the house and to safety. But once outside they realized that they had somehow miscounted. Young John Wesley, age five, was still in the house standing at an upstairs window. As the fire raged throughout the house the boy looked helplessly down at his panicked parents. It was too far for the boy to jump, but the house was now so engulfed in flames that no one could go in and hope to come out alive again.

One of the Wesley's neighbors awoken by the commotion, saw young John standing at the window. He immediately rushed over to the house directly beneath the window where the boy stood. He then placed his hands against the smoldering side of the house. Another neighbor saw what he was doing and quickly raced over to him, climbing atop his shoulders and also placing his hands against the house. Another neighbor did the same. This repeated until a human ladder had been formed and the last man- smashed the window to bring young John out of the raging inferno.

When Susanna Wesley held her son she said, "Surely you are a brand plucked from the fire!"

How could those men know that they held in their hands, the father of the Methodist movement? Did they comprehend that from this fiery preacher countless nations were born. *10th October 2013*

CHAPTER 10

I AM ASKING, "LORD, BE MY FRIEND?"

PRAYER, Early, at midnight I prayed a moving prayer:

"LET ALL THE WISHES, DESIRES, EXPECTATIONS, anticipations and imaginations of all my enemies turn to me into great force of blessings to cause me to go forth to Win Souls from all colours, languages and nations for the Lord. Also, may all the curses against me turn into blessings. Let all the four pregnant cows, every cow which will or would have produced from now on, be counted and turn into blessings. I ask the cause my prayers to be heard and answered to bring millions of Souls into the Kingdom of God. Amen." *1st March 2014*

I RECEIVED NEWS THAT TWO MORE OF MY COWS DISAPPEARED from kraal. I woke up Clare, Loy and RPG we bombarded the gates of heaven and within 30 minutes I received another call from Julius that they had appeared. *23rd May 2014*

I WOKE UP AND PRAYED TO GOD ABOUT MY SON ROBERT. Remembering Joseph and what Jacob went through all those years without hope after his sons had lied him that his son was eaten by animals yet a surprise was waiting for him. Robert went on his own, he is a big boy.

I prayed to God about if there was anything, I said which annoyed him. Then I remembered a story of a lady who annoyed her best friend. A lady one day said something which annoyed her valued friend very much and was afraid that their friendship was going to break up. She went to seek advise from a wise old woman. The wise old woman listened to her story and gave her advise to get a pillow full of feathers, early in the morning before people wake up, run to every house on the village place on every door a single feather, after that come and report to me. The young lady did as the old wise woman told her. She got a pillow full of feathers very early in the morning she started to run around the village until she placed a single feather on every door without leaving one door till day break. She was so exhausted. She went back to the old woman and reported that she emptied the pillow after placing every feather on each door in the village. The old wise woman asked her to wake up again early in the morning before everybody woke up to go and pick those feathers and fill the pillow again.

The young lady said, "Alas!!! Every feather as I was placing them immediately the wind blew and carried them away!! I can't find even one!" Then the old wise woman replied "As you spoke those words to your friend that is how the wind carried them away.

This is how the old wise lady treated the broken heart of the young lady, she made her work hard and at risk to restore her friendship.

So, I asked the Lord also to carry away every word that got into the heart of Robert and annoyed him to the extent of running away. *9th June 2014*

I WOKE UP AT 1.00AM STARTED TO PRAY WITH INTERCESSION spirit about the spirits attacking me. Again, I prayed the prayer that I prayed on 28th February 2014 after when I learnt that my two other cows were stolen again.

Prayer, Lord may all the prayers, curses, condemnations, desires, expectations, anticipations and imaginations of all my enemies turn into great spiritual blessings, and cause the result of my answered prayers to Win Souls for the Lord. That I may cause a great vacuum on the kingdom of Satan by emptying hell to fill heaven. That every time my enemies think, wish and imagine evil against me let that cause me to grow stronger with blessings to go forth to win souls of every colour, language and nation from all four corners of the world. Let the devil's kingdom be affected by an exodus of souls which are leaving until he'll go to join heaven as the Word of God is the one which is spear heading all my prayers. Lord! When any one gets a job done or accomplishes a task, he expects a reward. Also, for me now after all what I have been going through, I expect a reward, and I ask may My reward be my prayers be answered for seeking Souls of men and women to be won from the jaws of the evil one. Souls of every colour, languages and nations from all four corners of the world. *19th June 2014*

I FINISHED MY FASTING JOURNEY OF NO DELICACIES AND ON.

23rd June 2019

Polycarp was a second-century bishop of Smyrna, in the western region of modern-day Turkey. When the authorities decided to execute him, he refused to flee. When he was brought into the stadium, the proconsul pled with the elderly man to renounce his faith but Polycarp declared, "Eighty and six years have I served him, and he never did me any injury; how then can I blaspheme my King and my Savior?" The proconsul threatened to burn him alive, but Polycarp replied: "You threaten me with fire which burns for an hour, and after a little is extinguished, but are ignorant of the fire of the coming judgment and of eternal punishment, reserved for the ungodly. But why do you tarry? Bring forth what you will." When the fire did not touch Polycarp, he was stabbed to death. And so, he died for the One who died for him.

None of us can truly know if we will die for Jesus until such a moment comes. Corrie ten Boom's dad said it, when Corrie as a little girl and put it before his dad that I want to be a Christian but what I fear is to die as a martyr. We may not face martyrdom but we can each decide if we will live for him today. *26th June 2014*

Neepu/CIS, I am in travail like a woman in labour to give birth to a child in the world.

We have cried tears and tears but only the Lord wipes them away. *27th June 2014*

I woke up at 4.30pm with insight saying that young people as they grow, they set a goal. They think straight ahead and work towards that goal, e.g. studying, money, education, being known or by that being on top of everybody that is all they want. They do not consider that in reaching that goal, there will be obstacles, hurdles to jump and huddles to group. Some goals are so dangerous they carry death penalties. Many young people die, before they reach that Big Goal they have set.

I cried and asked the Lord, "Why in the World one can search and try to find one trusted person and finds none?" I have tried so many people, if you find one trusted, he or she is a thief, if he or she is not a thief they do not have the qualifications for your expectations. If he or she has your expectations but can be a liar, a traitor, or hiding in faith to use it as cover up.

I realized that one day God Himself asked "Whom can I send" and Isaiah said "Send me Lord!" Isaiah 6:8. God created all people in the World but who could He ask such a question? Could He fail to pick any one to send?

Another time the Lord said "I have looked into the whole World to find who can stand in the Gap that I may not destroy the land," Ezekiel 22:30. Really? God Himself, whose world and all its people are, who has all people in His hands, was looking for only one to stand in the Gap.

Here is the answer, God has all Wisdom in His workings. He created man with a Free Will to decide which to do, as right or wrong Period. He did not create Robots. However, man has a choice to make out on his own free Will. That is where the source of problem is coming from because man can choose to follow God without being coerced or can choose to follow the devil, he has this freedom. Yes, in the whole World there can be not one whole heartedly following God. Either they are following God because there is something they are looking for, e.g. money, publicity, healing, women, men, etc. The Lord said that they are looking for Me because of bread.

My prayer, I said Lord please brew and blend within me your Word, let it saturate in me so that I will be full of your Word to lead, guide and direct me always. Let life be given to me as Esther of old who prayed for her life from king Xerxes. The life in its fulness to serve You, that whenever You look around You will say "at least Kabatalemwa is there." Even if the World denies You, I will Accept you, and bring Smiles on your Face. Let me be pure and a clean Field where if one tries to throw garbage, they will be ashamed and pick it himself. Because that I will desire nothing except to do your Will. Amen.

In 2010 and for a long time the Lord was more vivid when I was on 45 days honey and water fast. He asked me "ask what do you want me to do for you." I asked everything I thought of as important, but still He continued to asked me the same question because when I thought I had not given Him a favorable answer. This time after addressing all those points above again, I laid my head down and said "Lord, when you asked king Solomon the same question and king Solomon answered You were wonderful. Lord, I am young Give me understanding. You told king Solomon that because he did not have asked for enemies to die, riches or long life, but have asked for Wisdom. So, I am giving you wisdom, 1 Kings 3:5-13. So, for me today on 30th June 2014 I am asking, Lord, be my friend?" *30th June 2014*

CHAPTER 11
WHAT IS A PLATE?

I WOKE up at 3.12am opened the Bible and read about Zephaniah's prophesy that a great day of the Lord's wrath on mankind was near when there be judgment on Judah's enemies, Jerusalem and all nations. All them can call on God and He will answer and judge them along with Israel. Then the darkness will be made light and Israel will rejoice with praise for their restorations, Zephaniah 1-3.

There were three delivery trips of sand put on the Secondary school building site. That is the First step to start a most exciting journey.
1st July 2014

I READ ABOUT THE INHERITANCE BATTLE BETWEEN JACOB and Esau that was set on the Gaza strip where God's people could not land even after 40 years in the wilderness and had to pass through, but not without a Fight with king Sihon of Heshbon, Deuteronomy 2. *2nd July 2014*

Dream, I had invited a few senior Pastors for a dinner, which was ready on the table. We prayed after praying for the food, when I went to get plates to serve them, I found the plates which I had thought were clean and in order, I found they were all dirty. The children kept them as we had used them earlier, they are many, many, plates, but all dirty, every one we picked, some had the previous left over of chicken legs. We were three people cleaning plates but every one we would clean was getting dirty again. I picked a dish and served cassava mixed with beans, but still I looked for the plates, they were not there. I could not carry it to them, so I came back to the children to get clean plates but they were still dirty.

Interpretation, I have been organizing Pastors, Seminars and inviting facilitators (plates) to serve food (the Word of God) to the Pastors but they are not clean.

What is a plate? A plate is a container where you serve food and source ready to be consumed. Spiritual Pastors are the spiritual leaders in the church. A sitting Room, is where people can hold family discussions and/or eat. A meal here is the Word of God. A plate represents a vessel where one is handing over the food.

In spirit, the plate is a vessel you use to serve Word of God.

This reminded me of another dream I had some time back that I was having a place of chips and all other good things on my plate, I was near the ocean shore, I stumbled and my plate fell over the ocean and so then many plates multiplied into thousands of plates and started floating on the furthest corners of the ocean.

3rd July 2014

At 5.40am I opened to read the Word of God.

Message, it is He that sitteth upon the circle of the earth, and the inhabitants thereof are as grasshoppers; that stretcheth out the heavens as a curtain, and spreadeth them out as a tent to dwell in: That bringeth the princes to nothing; he maketh the judges of the earth as vanity. Yea, they shall not be planted; yea, they shall not be sown: yea, their stock shall not take root in the earth: and he shall also blow upon them, and they shall wither, and the whirlwind shall take them away as stubble. To whom then will ye liken me, or shall I be equal? saith the Holy One. Lift up your eyes on high, and behold who hath created these things, that bringeth out their host by number: he calleth them all by names by the greatness of his might, for that he is strong in power; not one faileth. ... He giveth power to the faint; and to them that have no might he increaseth strength. Even the youths shall faint and be weary, and the young men shall utterly fall: But they that wait upon the Lord shall renew their strength; they shall mount up with wings as eagles; they shall run, and not be weary; and they shall walk, and not faint, Isaiah 40:22-31 (KJV). *10th July 2014*

Medical Mission to Nyamabuga Foundation Schools

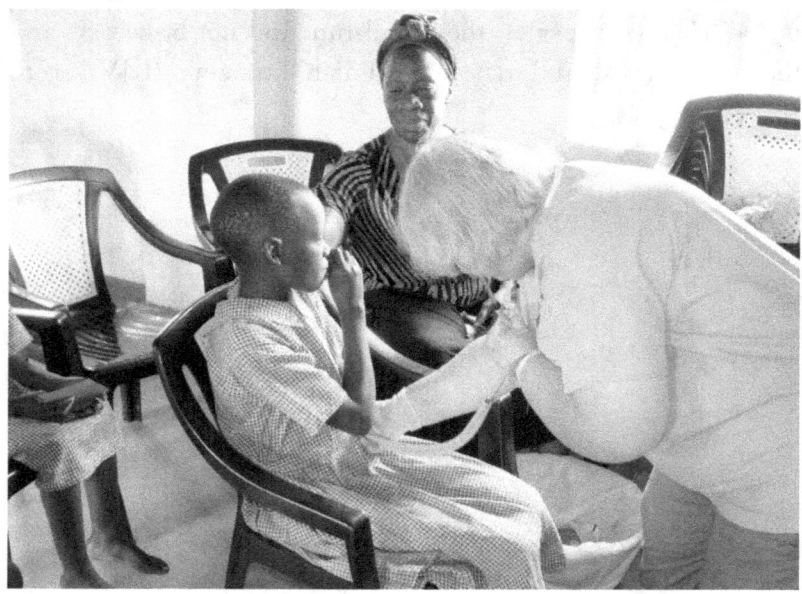

CHAPTER 12

NO COMPROMISE

PRAISE AND WORSHIP was so strong I went to join the children. After some 30 minutes elapsed, I wanted to withdraw and stand alone by the road going to the Secondary but had three people joining, and the girl from the kitchen. After like a few minutes I heard shrieking voice and the children scattered shouting as if there was danger. I ran back and found one of the girls rolling on the ground, and I started chasing her rebuking the devil up to the fence. We battled with the enemy until after like an hour until when she was exhausted. Some devils left.

She came and complained that her chest was heavy and she could not laugh. I told her I was going pray for her but I was a bit busy till the time of evening prayer came. I was sitting with a brother when the praise and worship started, again I heard the shrieking voice and the children continued praising. I escorted the brother then I went to join the kids and I found a few people in the middle of the circle holding two girls who were kind of entangled together. I told them to separate them. I took Karungi and concentrated my attention on her until she calmed down and settled down. Then I went to the one who was raging, I started to rebuke the devil for over an hour until we managed to cause her to call the name of Jesus Christ, then it was 9.00pm.

Start voluntary fast and had service with the kids. *17th July 2014*

A RELATIVE OF MINE, CAME TO VISIT ME SAYING THAT SHE was convicted to come to me to tell her the truth of Salvation and she said that I leave nothing out. In actual fact she was not meaning it, there was something she was concealing because she was not ready to take. I shared with her the Scripture of Jeremiah and the men of Israel who went with the same attitude, and the Lord fore told him they were coming to see him, but were lying, they were not meaning what they were saying.

When I pointed to her the issue of Tooro King Kamurasi and his Godliness, how pioneered Tooro into a Godly Kingdom and her husband who succeeded him how he took back the Kingdom to idolatry and fornication and the kingdom backslid she was not ready for that piece of information, she got annoyed and said King Rukidi had love.

In my reply I said one can have only love but committing other abominable sins, which can erase love. It's not only one good attribute which can covers the multitude of sins.

People are condoning sin, even when they are told they want to cover (Tooro Sswekerra, Butikira principal), God does not want that, He wants to expose sin so that it is uprooted once and for all. If you want to work for God be serious with His principals, no compromise and condoning spirit.

22nd July 2014

I changed my voluntary fast to water/honey. In prayer I learnt that a friend does not kill you, he takes you with him; but an enemy kills you. Therefore, when people of God die, they say: they have rested, they have departed or they have gone, etc. But when the people who do not know the Lord die, they say they have died. *24th July 2014*

CHAPTER 13

GIVE TIME TO DAILY PRAYER

A Covenant of Salt is a perpetual or everlasting covenant - probably due to salt's preserving properties. An increase in the anointing of the gift of discernment.

ANNA ROUNTREE

WHEN A PERSON IS able to see coming disasters in the future or unconfessed sin in another's life, one feels some measure of the pain experienced by our Lord. The Lord instructed Anna do not touch your nose. Because there was flames and salt in Anna's hands. The nose means discerning, it is a prophetic gift, a huge gift for pastors and those in Ministry, and it is controlled by the Holy Spirit.

One day Bob said just right "out of the blue" that it was hard for prophets to die. "There is so much light and life in their bones," he answered. "It is hard for them to die." He then related the Biblical story of the body of a deceased man hastily thrown into the grave of Elisha the prophet. When the deceased man touched the bones of Elisha he came back to life and walked away. I prayed.

Heaven Awaits vision of Anna Rountree, Denise.

If someone says "God seems very far away," Ask, who moved? When not getting an answer to a prayer some people believe that means they didn't get the answer they wanted, but the answer is there. Sometimes the answer to the prayer is "No" and it may come in the form of silence, but we think God doesn't hear us. We definitely can be very good at self-sabotage. If we are asking God to change an aspect or character, attitude in ourselves, and we are not personally committed to that change, it may not happen or there might be no visible results.

Sometimes we want God to work within our time frame, and when He is working within His time frame. "God, I need to hear from you by such and such a date or time." Sometimes when we believe God isn't answering us, what might be needed is giving up our time frame for His time frame, and a time when we need to ground ourselves in our greatest and most sincere patience. Sometimes "His" answer is right in front of us and we are just not seeing it.

If we are asking God to change an aspect of ourselves, e.g. stop getting angry, stop an addiction, stop feeling victim, or a number of things, if we are not personally and fully committed to that change it very well may not happen. We can also be fully committed to it for the wrong reasons. God wants to help us. But if we are asking for the wrong things, or our motives are not pure, we may not hear an answer. I try to remember to ask for things according to His will, not mine and God doesn't need to have us do it all perfectly and He only answers those prayers presented in a perfect manner because God is God.

For me, I find that when I voice my prayer toward the change needed in me, it seems the prayer is heard more fully and more quickly, e.g. I need to walk in your presence or to see more clearly in the spirit. When I pray instead of asking Him to "fix" or "change" another person or situation I phrase the prayer in a way that asks, "God, what am I not seeing in this prayer answer?" e.g. Peter 22 years, Robert 11 years, what is my part that I should change, do I need to have faith and patience? How could this situation possibly be serving or helping You? When God seems quiet, either He doesn't hear us, or he does but is ignoring us, then I ask, Lord, please help me see this situation more clearly and have understanding and clarity of action because I got no response. I usually put a fleece.

Time should be given daily to prayer. For me, it is my quiet time with God, my personal intimate time with God. And sometimes what is best for me to just to shut up and listen. Sometimes we are so busy we do not shut up long enough or stop spinning long enough to hear or notice God's answer. So, I very much agree, distractions can cause a potentially strong prayer to just stop.

If you abide in Me, and My words abide in you, you will ask for what you desire and it shall be done for you, John 15:7.

And whatever we ask we receive from Him because we keep His commandments and do those things which are pleasing in His sight, 1 John 3:22. We do not earn answers to prayers just, we cannot earn our salvation which only comes through faith. Our prayers are answered through His grace and mercy.

Jesus gave his disciples an outline for prayer where He councils that when we pray, we go to a quiet room, close the door, and pray in secret; and not to heap up empty phrases of many words, for your Father knows what you need before you ask Him. Then Jesus recites for them our Lord's Prayer, Mathew 6:5-13. Prayer isn't simply asking or "begging" of God, rather, it is about believing in God.

Therefore I say to you, whatever things you ask when you

pray believe that you receive them and you will have them, Mark 11:23. When praying, believe in the final results of the prayer, it may or may not happen immediately. i.e. Peter experience after 22 years, but believe you will experience that tangible gift. If not immediately today, it may be at a later time, but believe you will receive because you will. And if the issue involves dealing with some satanic or demonic person, you need to call on assistance. I am not any sort of expert here, but what I do know is to invoke the name of Jesus Christ and that empowers you with the authority to deal with such entities, Mark 13:34. And, Please, if you have any sort of Situation involving the "dark side" which I summarize these issues into, please contact someone knowledgeable in these matters.

We need Faith, Belief, Patience, Persistence and no doubts. Sometimes people do give up too early when, all they had to do was place one foot in front of the other. We never know what is just around the next corner. I feel like I could write a book here, but I will stop for now because I know some people do not appreciate the posts that go on, and on, and on. I for one, so I've been praying to God to help me be more mindful of that.

Reviewing my prayer from 13th February 2011, "The cloud of Unknowing." God unto whom all hearts be open and unto whom no secret thing is hid, I beseech thee, so for to cleanse the intent of my heart with the unspeakable gift of Thy Grace, that I may perfectly love You and worthily praise You. Amen.

Prayer is effective or powerful but when it is not answered something is wrong either it is prayed in negative or it becomes ineffective, James 4:3. Furthermore, to pray effectively we must pray within the context of the world situation as God sees it, not what the world thinks about itself with abortions, gays, etc. Human should have Rights that should influence us, but what God thinks about the World. Rotten.

> *Prayer, oh, God let thy Glory be revealed once more to men; through me if it please You or without me or a part from me, it matters not. Restore Thy church to the place of moral beauty that becomes as the Bride of Christ; through me or a part from me, only let this prayer be answered. O! God, honour who. Thou will. Let me be used or overlooked or ignored. Amen.*

No man is worthy to succeed until he is willing to Fail. No man is worthy to be a success in spiritual activities until he is willing that the honour of succeeding should go to another. If God so Wills, i.e. John the Baptist.

God will allow His servant to succeed when He has learned that success does not make him dearer to God, nor more valuable in the total scheme of things. Our great honour lies in being just what Jesus was and is. To be accepted by those who accept Him, rejected by all who reject Him, loved by those who love Him and hated by everyone that hates Him.

What a terrible thing for men and women to get old and have no hope or prospects and no gracious promise for the long eternity before them. *25th July 2014*

CHAPTER 14

HE WILL HAVE PEOPLE WHO WILL PRAISE, PRAY AND WORSHIP

FOR A LONG TIME I have been wondering why I have attracted rejection from every corner even a person walking on the street. Right from the time I came to know the Lord, I was accused of being over serious over this issue of salvation. My mum, and others were asking themselves why I was not getting married when I was still looking young and beautiful.

What has rendered people of God ineffective and tied His hands not to work, people have been invaded by a spirit of compromise. They say "Everyone is doing it. Who is? not me!" They see God very far away because they do not see, touch, taste or hear. They distance Him, and say God seems to be far. Ask yourself Who moved? He is ever present. When you are over serious with the things of God and one is in a compromising spirit, every time he or she will be convicted or guilty; even if you say nothing to point at their mistake. *26th July 2014*

PRAYER, LORD YOUR SPIRIT OF PROPHESY WAS ON MOSES,

Elijah, Elisha, Joseph, Daniel, Isaiah, Jeremiah, etc. Also we have people who have lived and died in these centuries they did what pleased you. These people walked on the same soil we are walking, ate the same food we are eating they felt sleep, they felt tired like any one of us but served you honestly. Lord I am asking: why have people of this generation especially in Africa no person has stood to serve you as these men and women in the 18th Century, 19th Century, 20th Century and now in the 21st Century. People like John Wesley, Smith Wigglesworth, Mary Etter, Katherine Khulman, William Seymour, Aimee MacPerson, and Billy Graham.

My declaration was: this place will always have people who will Praise, Pray and Worship in Spirit and truth. *10th August 2014*

THE WORLD IS STEEPED IN SIN, AND REBELLION AGAINST God. It is time for God to punish mankind. We must turn from our wicked ways and grieve as God grieves over our sins. The nations most blessed, but also the most wicked, will be the first ones punished. No one should rejoice at the demise of any nation, because their turn is coming. *20th August 2014*

DECLARATION, AS LONGER AS I PRAISE AND WORSHIP THE Lord in Spirit and Truth, love the Lord deeply and be in union in spirit, I walk in His present: healing will take place spiritually and physically from the crown of my head to the soul of my feet for every ailment.

Burial of Abooki Nyakato, in the Sermon Richard Baguma

said in Nigerian three brothers were walking when they found a bag of money and picked it. They thought how they were going to distribute it among themselves, but realized their little brother was talkative he would reveal the secret of how they got the money. They hitched a plan: that they send their little brother to the shops to buy food for them to eat, that when he returns, they kill him to keep his mouth shut. Also, the little brother at the shop thought how his brothers hated him so much, they might try to kill him, he bought the poison and put it in the food. So, when he arrived with the food, they grabbed him and killed him, and they sat down to eat their meal. They all three died and that was the end of their lives and the money no one benefitted from it. *29th August 2014*

DREAM, I SAW A HUGE LIVE FIGURE IT HAD OVAL SHAPE. I asked someone invisible and powerful that: There is something so powerful which I am seeing in the spirit which is going to be born on one side of the world and another from opposite side. What effect are they going to cause to the world? He said there has been already three powers which came but people did not Notice which shook the world and have already done damage.

The Bulldozer came and the men started on leveling, my heart rested.

Children resumed school.

1st September 2014

AT LEAST IT DID NOT RAIN THE WHOLE DAY, WE DID GENERAL cleaning and later went to the Ranch. I visited the site and found where the Lord led me to pray and anoint before the excavation started. The boy worker had dug out stones and a pot out of the ground. *6th September 2014*

The way to find yourself is to lose yourself in the service of others.
They did not leave you when you were young so do not leave them when they are old!!! 9th September 2014

I WOKE UP ASKING THE LORD A SIGN THAT HE HAS ALLOWED The unbelievers to help me in His Works. I was led to read: Arise, shine, for your light has come, and the glory of the LORD has risen upon you. ... "For behold, I create new heavens and a new earth, Before they call I will answer; while they are yet speaking I will hear. But be glad and rejoice forever in that which I create; for behold, I create Jerusalem to be a joy, and her people to be a gladness, Isaiah 60 and 65:16-25 (ESV), amazing Grace.

Prayer, The city of the Lord, The Zion of the Holy One of Israel, Isaiah 60:14 (KJV).

Lord, let me be Your City, and the Zion of the Holy One of Israel.

CHAPTER 15

A SPIRITUAL MEASURING LINE

READ entire Romans 5 and What I learnt in this scripture:

Verse 1, We are made right in God's sight by faith in His promises. We can have real peace with Him because of what Jesus Christ has done for us.

Verse 2, Because of our faith He has brought us in His highest place where we can now stand and confidently and joyfully look forward to be all what God has had in mind for us to be.

Verse 3, When we run into problems and trials, we know they are good for us because they help us to be thoughtful and patient and lead us to pray.

Verse 4, Patience which develops strength of character in us and helps us to trust God more until our hope and faith are strong and steady, e.g. my experiences of Peter and Robert.

Verse 5, When all this happens, we hold our heads high, no matter what happens and know that all is well, for we know how dearly God loves us, we feel this warm love every

Verse 6, When we were helpless dead in sin without escape Jesus came and died for us sinners.

Verse 8, God showed His great love by sending Christ to die for us while we were still sinners.

Verse 9, He declared us not guilty, and saved us from God's wrath to come.

Verse 10, When we were God's enemies we were brought back to God by the death of Christ, and now we are His friends and He is living within us.

Verse 11, Because of what Jesus Christ did for us making us friends of God now we are rejoicing in a wonderful new relationship with God.

Verse 12: When Adam sinned, sin entered the entire human race. His sin spread death the whole world so everything began to grow old and die.

Verse 13, People were sinning from the time of Adam until Moses time. God did not judge them guilty of death for breaking His Law, because He had not yet given His Laws to them, nor told them what He wanted them to do.

Verse 14, So, when their bodies died it was Not for their own sins, since they themselves had never disobeyed God's special law agaist eating the for hidden fruit as Adam did.

(nahabweki emibiri yabo obu yafiire, atabe habwebibi byabo, nobu habwabo tibali nubo bajemiire iteeka lya Ruhanga habwokulya Eki ekijuma ekyali kibatangirwe nka Adam.

Verse 15, What a contrast between Adam and Christ who was yet to come. And what a difference between Man's sin and God's forgiveness! Adam brought a curse and death to mankind but Christ brought Blessings and life to mankind through God's mercy.

Verse 20, God gave ten Commandments in order for mankind to look at himself in a mirror and see their failure to obey God's laws. The more we see our sinfulness, the more we see God's abounding grace to forgive us this day.

Early in the morning I stopped the casting of concrete and

called Charles Turyatunga to come and check the men on the site. He came and found a mess. Mukiibi had appointed the Foreman who does not even know how to interpret the plan. Clare came and brought the Blue Prints. Charles came to visit the site. Burial of Ronnie's grandmother.

The Lord showed me a spiritual insight of A Spiritual Measuring Line. God has put a line where to measure spiritual standards. That's why many people are against you who is trying to measure to the Standards of God. Where there is no truthfulness, faithfulness the line cuts through, if it is the head, the hand, the leg or half way people are left with anger, hatred, jealousy and devastated cause no one wants to accept his weakness, except to hate you.

When Jesus Christ came, He came with a measuring line which devastated the works of the devil which were operating in the Pharisees, Sadducees and Scribes, when the line passed through them, they hated Him so much to the extent of killing Him. *2nd October 2014*

CHAPTER 16

LORD CLOTHE ME WITH A ROBE OF PRAYER

AFTER PRAYER WALK, I was meditating the Lord spoke to me about the 40ft full container that He wants to give me wrapped up dynamic power. As I walked in the kitchen Emma said he had a dream for me about containers full of goods and did not know who sent them, but I was called to sign the papers. I learnt about the death of a friend's grandson death on the beach. *16th September 2014*

As I was reminiscing about the death of my friend's boy. I was so uncomfortable on the floor. I developed a prayer in the line of this discomfort.

Prayer, Lord you are the one who made me leave the comfort of my bed to let me sleep on this hard floor since 1988. You knew what was going to be accomplished. Therefore, let all the hurt and discomfort I have been and continued experiencing be wrapped into such dynamic power in the city of my soul You have built with souls of men, that it will go forth to win souls of men of every colour, race and language on all the continents of the world. Let this wrapped power be transformed in a spiritual New Clear War Head, to go and smash, crash and demolish every satanic power from above, on ground and in heavenilies. which stands to block the power of God to work in men.

Let this be a wrapped dynamic power: blow up all the rocks which have stood in the souls of men when I pray let it make bridges in the souls of men to cross over from the enemy's Camp to Your Camp. Let it make high ways in the souls of men to come to you where there was no way. Let there always be something to give spiritually, physcally and materially everyone even if it is a smile to my enemies. Let this power mend the torn-up souls which were like rags.

Let it treat the wounded hearts. Let it level down high mountains and fill up the valleys in the souls of men, Lord, the precedent prayer it has been going on since 1987 but to date it has been increasing from strength to strength especially on 1st January 2007, when I was at Kasozi Prayer Mountain when one person said he claimed 1000 souls for a year. I intercede for the babies born every second in the world. I intercede for those still rebellious every second hurting God in idolatry, paganism, and satanism. I intercede for those dying every second to meet the Lord on their journey through prayer.

I asked the Lord that every Word and prayer I send over the universe to meet these people of every colour, language and race to create towers and alters on every continent of the world which are going to make a strong force to crash satan's empire. The Lord came and fought the battle and left us with power and authority to overcome satan him and his demons. When the Lord left, He gave power to those who try to experience His nearness or create His closeness by moving, and being close to God.

We need to think about God, and Holy thinking creates a moral climate favourable to the growth of faith, love and humility and reverence. We need Spirit inspired thinking which helps us to make our minds pure sanctuaries in which God will be pleased to dwell. Vision, illustration of a Raven and a dove in Noah's Ark.

We should train our thoughts by long periods of daily prayer. Long practice in the art of mental prayer that is talking to God inwardly as we work or travel. This will form the habit of Holy Thoughts. *17th September 2014*

> Message, the Lord said: "People not seeing me does not mean that I am not there, I am there, then they are there, because I am Omnipotent, Omnipresent and Omniscient.

KANGUME GAVE ME A REPORT THAT ON 19TH, THERE WAS A large python which was in the swamp the whole day people were spectating the huge python. Therefore, You, God, saved our kids from the danger of a python. *21st September 2014*

PRAYER, THAT THE LORD CLOTHE ME WITH A ROBE OF prayer, praise, worship, repentance and accepting Him daily. This is what is going to keep me working Holy before Him. I prayed that let the Altar and Tower of Prayer I have built over years start emitting sparks of fire according to the strength and magnanimity the enemy hordes come to attack me, even when I am sleeping or in recesses.

Let the sparks go in form of New Clear War Heads into far

lands and oceans on water and under water, Go like Long Range Ballistic Missiles to hit in the places of Aliens, Principalities and Rulers of the Air on planets and Air, Go like Atomic Bombs which hit Hiroshima and Nagasaki on the land. Let them go like Bull Dozers to bulldoze the satanic powers on ground and underground into the Dead Sea. *27th September 2014*

Kangume Stella

CHAPTER 17

THOUGHTS

IN THIS WORLD we are living, our lives are driven by thoughts which are Good or evil, constructive or destructive, developmental or domant. When your life is driven by clear, pure and holy thoughts you will have a direction, like a compass on of a ship on the big ocean and an aircraft in the outer space to its last destination.

On this day I learnt of the death of a friend, who was very much a live the previous day but was dead the next morning. Her son who was very sick all the time to the point of death is still a live. I thought human beings should take care of their lives daily by having clear, pure lives because one can never know the day you are going. *1st October 2014*

I WOKE UP AT 5.00AM AND I HAD A MOVING UNIVERSAL prayer for languages, colours and nations.

5th October 2014

THE LORD LED ME TO READ ISAIAH 55, EMPHASIS ON 3-6 - God's love is calling all nations to call on Him. I Prayed to the Lord to bring us an Administrator from any continent who has no conditions but led totally by the Spirit of God. *8th October 2014*

AND THE ENEMY WAS RACING DOWN TO BETH-HORON THE Lord destroyed them with great hail storm, more men died from the hail storm than by the swords of Israelites. The Lord Can Fight With Natural Calamity. Joshua prayed aloud; the Lord stopped the sun at Gibeon and the Moon at Aijalon. They never moved until the the Israel army had finished the destruction of its enemies. There had never been a day before, there had never been another since, when the Lord stopped the sun and moon all because of prayer of one man, Joshua 10:11-14.

For the Lord made the enemy kings want to Fight the Israelis instead of asking for Peace so they were mercilessly killed as the Lord has commanded Moses. Because the Lord wanted Joshua to rout all of the giants the descendants of Anak who lived in the hill country cities, Joshua 10:20.

The Lord allows our enemies not to ask for Pardon or not to be forgiven so that they can be punished. *11th October 2014*

CYNTHIA SENT ME AN EMAIL, I RECOGNIZED IT AS AN answer from the Lord, after asking Him so many times. Cynthia's message: The Lord will sustain you with His mighty right hand! He goes before You and has not forgotten all that He intends to do in and through you. Stand firm, dear friend, and be encouraged that He sees you, loves you and is well pleased with you. Not only what you have done and are doing but all that you Are pleases Him! He sees your heart and loves you deeply. So do I. *16th October 2014*

THE ISSUE OF MONEY SHOULD NOT BOTHER ME

At 11.00pm I received a call from a Moslem and a half Arab, he was drunk and started telling me that the issue of money should not bother me. He repeated it more than three times.

God used a donkey to talk to Balaam and a cock to confirm to Peter when he denied the Lord. The Lord told the Pharisees that He could make the stones praise Him when they were stopping people worshipping Him on His way to Jerusalem. *13th October 2011*

School courtyard

Baby class

CHAPTER 18

INFLUENCE

AT HOME ALL DAY. I Read 21 Laws, Joshua and the Law of Influence. Time needed to deepen influence. A mentor is required. Moses was the mentor of Joshua.

Leadership is Influence, the measure of leadership is influence - nothing more nothing less. Joshua failed to influence the people to follow his lead.

Leaders do not possess influence in all areas. Though Joshua was a leader but his influence did not out weigh the 11 tribal leaders which resulted into rebelliousness and punishment from God. The ten leaders that spread a bad report died there and then of plague before the Lord. and all their followers died in the desert, Numbers 14:36-37.

Influence can either be positive or negative, if the 12 spies had all given a good report of the Promised Land, the people of Israel would not have been led astray to suffer another 38 years in the wilderness. Influence is a two-edged sword, it cuts both positively or negatively. The 11 leaders led the Israelites astray, disaster for for those leaders and for all of their followers, even for

Moses, Joshua and Caleb, for all had to return to the wilderness for another 40 years, Numbers 14:26-35.

Faithful Leaders use Influence to add value. Joshua and Caleb wanted to motivate the Israelites to what would benefit everyone which is the agenda of great leaders.

With Influence comes Responsibility, a leader has to take a lead and live by example it's not commanding but Showing example that you can also do it, if you find a door left open do not pass by and order but Your subordinate to close it. Close it yourself.

Ineffective leaders give up. A good leader seeks to become a better leader despite set backs. Joshua continued to be faithful to God to learn as much as he could from Moses.

Influence grows with a good Mentor, through good mentorship you polish your skills. Moses imparted authority to Joshua and people accepted him because of Moses' training, Deuteronomy 31:7.

Influence grows with time and maturity, the difference in Numbers Joshua was still young and in Joshua he had matured and was skilled after walking with Moses, Numbers 14:1-10 and Joshua 18:1-10.

Influence of timing. One place cannot give you wisdom. With time we need the followers to go somewhere, see and assess. The Israelites had over stayed in the wilderness and had seen nothing except the sand. Take time is very important. When a message comes, do not delay that I will do it tomorrow.

Influence of Patience and Integrity, Joshua and Caleb through no fault of theirs to return to the desert for another 40 years. They never disgruntled, complained or became cynical men. Throughout the journey they kept consistent and credible.

Influence of being right, a leader always tries to lead people in the right direction so how much people do not think that you are foolhardy and rash. Your statements should stand the test of time never changing. *22nd October 2014*

CHAPTER 19

WE HAVE THE OPPORTUNITY TO BECOME RADIANT CHRISTIANS

HORNETS, And ye went over Jordan, and came unto Jericho: and the men of Jericho fought against you, the Amorites, and the Perizzites, and the Canaanites, and the Hittites, and the Girgashites, the Hivites, and the Jebusites; and I delivered them into your hand. And I sent the hornet before you, which drave them out from before you, even the two kings of the Amorites; but not with thy sword, nor with thy bow, Joshua 24:12.

Hornets!!! God can use nature to Fight us if we are not in obedience to Him.

And Joshua wrote these words in the book of the law of God, and took a great stone, and set it up there under an oak, that was by the sanctuary of the Lord. And Joshua said unto all the people, Behold, this stone shall be a witness unto us; for it hath heard all the words of the Lord which he spake unto us: it shall be therefore a witness unto you, lest ye deny your God, Joshua 24:26-27 (KJV).

Stone!!! God uses nature to be witness if we obey or try to turn away from Him.

The great things God used for Joshua to Fight with, He caused Joshua to stop River Jordan from flowing until the Israelites passed. He caused Joshua to bring the walls of Jericho to crumble down by Going around them praising Him. He caused hailstone to Fight Israel's enemies, Joshua 10:11-14. He allowed Joshua to stop the sun at Gibeon and the moon at Aijalon. He sent Hornets to fright for Israel in a war without bow and arrows. He caused Joshua to set the stone to be a witness to Israel. 25th October 2014

THERE SHALL NOT ANY MAN BE ABLE TO STAND BEFORE THEE all the days of thy life: as I was with Moses, so I will be with thee: I will not fail thee, nor forsake thee. Be strong and of a good courage: for unto this people shalt thou divide for an inheritance the land, which I sware unto their fathers to give them. Only be thou strong and very courageous, that thou mayest observe to do according to all the law, which Moses my servant commanded thee: turn not from it to the right hand or to the left, that thou mayest prosper whithersoever thou goest. This book of the law shall not depart out of thy mouth; but thou shalt meditate therein day and night, that thou mayest observe to do according to all that is written therein: for then thou shalt make thy way prosperous, and then thou shalt have good success. Have not I commanded thee? Be strong and of a good courage; be not afraid, neither be thou dismayed: for the Lord thy God is with thee whithersoever thou goest, Joshua 1:5-9 (KJV). 26th October 2014

I STARTED TO PRAY AT 4.16AM, IT WAS A MOVING PRAYER FOR the P7 in particular, and the other needs up to 6.45am. Kangume joined me. Also, this time an unusual, random, shower of rain came down for almost two minutes came down. *1st November 2014*

THERE'S NO DOUBT THAT A SINGLE PERSON CAN CHANGE THE world. From John Wilkes Booth and Lee Harvey Oswald to Martin Luther King, Jr. and John Paul II history bears the fingerprints of key individuals whose actions changed everything. But if you want your life to benefit the world forever, you'll need more than courage and skill - you'll need divine inspiration.

King Solomon was by reputation the wisest man who ever lived. You would think a book containing his accumulated wisdom would be a bestseller from his day to ours. Such a book did in fact exist; it was called "the Book of the Acts of Solomon," 1 Kings 11:41. But it has vanished without a trace. Meanwhile, a tiny letter written by a prisoner on behalf of a runaway slave, the New Testament book of Philemon, has been studied for 20 centuries because the Holy Spirit inspired it.

Nothing you do today may make the news tomorrow. But everything you do today in obedience to God's Spirit will be recorded and rewarded forever. Whether God is calling you to feed hungry children, or to touch hungry souls, you have a Kingdom assignment of eternal significance. And your obedience will change your culture in ways you may not see this side of glory.

"One act of obedience is better than one hundred sermons," (Dietrich Bonhoeffer). What sermon will your life preach today?

A British computer scientist invented the World Wide Web

and William Seryour of Azusa Street started pentecostal. The Wright Brothers invented with the airplane.

Sowing to the Spirit is the best antidote or cure for depression, anxiety, and worry. One of the works of the Word of God is to act as a cleanser. It can rid our bodies of toxins and replace them with the life and peace of God. The mind and heart saturated with the Word of God becomes "armored" against the wiles of Satan. God's Word strengthens us and empowers us to fulfill the purposes that he has chosen to perform through us.

Heart Deposit, set aside time every day to soak your heart and mind in the Word of God. As you do, sow to the Spirit by reciting the words you are meditating going on back to your King. *2nd November 2014*

BALAAM AND KING SAGA OF CURSING ISRAEL, NO ONE MAY curse the one who has been blessed. God does not change, He does not repent on His Word and He does not lie. Numbers 23:24. *3rd November 2014*

KINGDOMNOMICS. WE HAVE THE OPPORTUNITY TO BECOME radiant Christians. Jesus is waiting to shine forth in us! And when that happens, our hearts will swell with joy as we see the hand of God at work in our lives and our circumstances. Are you consumed with having your life hidden in Jesus? Are you consumed with a passion to know him better? When we get to the point that nothing matters more than him, our lives gain sharp focus. Jesus Christ's light then shines through us in amazing ways. *10th November 2014*

*Nyamabuga Foundation Schools in 2018.
Our school has more than 400 students*

LEARN MORE AT WWW.NEEPUGANDA.ORG

ACKNOWLEDGMENTS

ANNA ROUNTREE *Heaven Awaits the Bride: A Breathtaking Glimpse of Eternity* Charisma Media, Jul 15, 2013
Unless otherwise indicated, all Scripture quotations are taken from the Holy Bible, King James Version - Public Domain Scripture quotations marked (ESV) ® Bible (The Holy Bible, English Standard Version®), copyright © 2001 by Crossway, a publishing ministry of Good News Publishers. Used by permission. All rights reserved."

Scripture quotations marked (NIV) are taken from the Holy Bible, New International Version®, NIV®. Copyright © 1973, 1978, 1984, 2011 by Biblica, Inc.™ Used by permission of Zondervan. All rights reserved worldwide. www.zondervan.com The "NIV" and "New International Version" are trademarks registered in the United States Patent and Trademark Office by Biblica, Inc.™

ABOUT THE AUTHOR

The late Gertrude Kabatalemwa labored for the kingdom of God in her native land of Uganda. The burden of her heart was for the good news of Jesus to become deeply rooted, firmly grounded, and abundantly fruitful in the lives of the people of Uganda. In the past, she has served her nation as secretary to the president. She also functioned as Minister for the Development of Women.

At one point, she had taken in thirty-five of the orphans into her own village home, subsequently establishing Nyamabuga Foundational Schools for village children. Her plans include to prepare and equip these young people with the skills necessary to be able to lead their nation with a moral worldview.

Today, her children and those that she has poured into continue her work.

Through this book, you will be blessed by encountering the very large heart of this precious servant of God.

This is Gertrude's sixth book of the series "My Deepest Heart's Devotions."

facebook.com/neepuganda

www.ingramcontent.com/pod-product-compliance
Lightning Source LLC
Chambersburg PA
CBHW052201110526
44591CB00012B/2037